A World of Java Programming

Marissa Walther & Shaun Flynn

Table of Contents

Introduction

In the world that we live in today, technology is a growing factor and influence in different jobs and lifestyles. People using phones, and computers to do their every day tasks, and companies running data bases to keep track of all their data; all come from code.

Code, seen as the basis of everything that functions in today's society, can be anything from the code of the human being (DNA) to the code that creates high end software. In a world where technology is becoming more vital, it is important to understand this new direction, and perhaps take a part in its development.

Everything starts at a beginning, and as you open this book for the first time you shall find an adventure that will lead you through the basis of a coding language called Java, all the way to using Java to create GUIs. The adventure that you will go on is one of trial and error, learning, and most of all, giving you the experience and the basis to understand the direction that the future is heading.

As you go through this book, we have prepared examples, example code, questions, and images that will all help you on your journey. We hope that you shall find your adventure to be successful, and we wish you the best of luck on your journey to becoming a programmer!

Chapter One:

Hello World

What is Java

Almost everything around us is ran by some type of program. From cars to dishwashers almost every device has a computer built into it. But what is a program, and what is a computer?

In computer science, a computer is any device that can store and manipulate data. In a traditional electronic computer data is stored in two locations: the hard drive (used for long-term storage) and the random-access memory (abbreviated RAM and used for short term storage). All memory in an electronic computer is stored as 0s and 1s. Theses 0s and 1s are called bits (short for binary digits). The computer manipulates the data in memory using its central processing unit (CPU). The CPU is the brains of the computer. Don't worry too much about how all of these systems work. You just need to have a basic understanding of them and know that they exist.

A program is a set of instructions that tell a computer how to manipulate the data that is stored in memory. For example, we could have a simple program that just adds two numbers in the RAM together. However, computers only understand the binary 0s and 1s (called machine language). So, talking to them and telling them what to do is tricky and hard to understand. Because of this, programmers have invented programming languages.

A programing language is a set of words and phrases that can be easily translated into machine language, so computers can understand it. There are many kinds of programing languages, and they all have their own strengths and weaknesses. The Java programing language is just one of these.

Java can be classified as a high level, object oriented, byte code interpreted programing language. That is a mouthful to say so let's break it down. A high-level language is any programing language that is relatively close to sounding like a real language (such as English). This makes it easier to look at and understand. An object-oriented language specializes in putting code in little packets called objects (these will be discussed in later sections of the book). Lastly, a byte code interpreted language doesn't automatically translate to machine language. Instead it goes to an intermediate language called byte code. This makes Java able to be run on any computer in the world that has Java installed on it. Most programing languages can't do this.

So the steps in Java programing are:

1. Create a code in Java (called source code)
2. Give the code to a compiler to turn into byte code
3. Run the code with any computer that has a Java Virtual Machine
4. The Virtual Machine translates the code for the computer
5. The computer does what the Virtual Machine tells it to do. The computer also "talks" to the Virtual Machine about what it is currently doing.

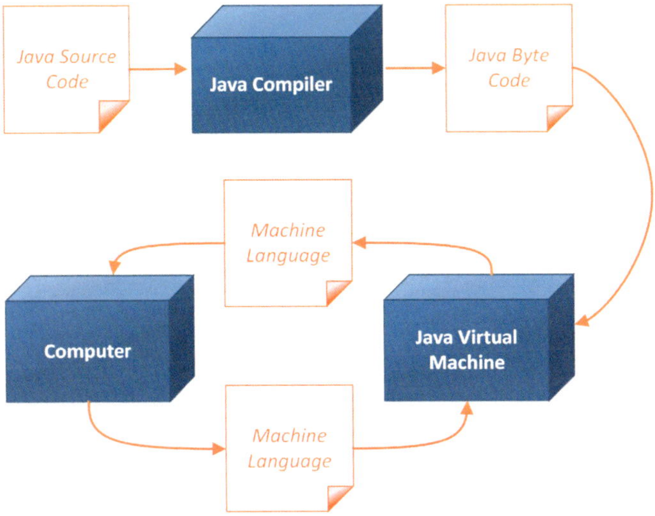

Setting Up Your Environment

Before you can start programming in Java, you will first need to get the Java SDK (Software Development Kit). This set of files contains everything Java will need to convert your programs to Java Byte Code. (See "How to Download Java")

Although it is possessible to write Java code using almost any simple text editor, there are professional programs that streamline the process of writing code. Called Integrated Development Environments (or IDEs), these programs include useful features like: spell checking, logic error detection, syntax error detection, built in compilers, and many more features.

There are many different IDEs out there and each one has its pros and cons. This book is designed to work well with either the Eclipse IDE or the IntelliJ IDE. We recommend looking at both and choosing the one that works best for you. Remember that your, decision is not set in stone, feel free to tryout one and switch if you don't like it.

The next two sections will show how to create your first program in Eclipse and Intellij respectively. Skip to the section that describes the IDE that you will be using.

Creating a Program In Eclipse

Once you have downloaded Eclipse it's time to create our first program. To start, open Eclipse and select the default workspace by selecting "OK" on the pop-up window. You will have to do this each time you open Eclipse.

The first time you open a new workspace you will be greeted by the Eclipse welcome screen. Here you can get an overview of the entire IDE along with a few simple tutorials. For now, just click the "restore" button at the top right corner of the screen.

Now that we have opened the Eclipse editor there are three important windows to take note of:

- Package Explorer: Located on the left-hand side of the screen, this is where we will see all of the projects (programs) that are saved to this particular workspace.

- The Editor Window: The large blank space in the center of the screen is the editor window. This will be used later to edit and create our code.

- The Console: The console can be found at the bottom of the screen under the console tab, this is where any print statements, errors, or other important information will be displayed when we run our programs. If the console isn't being displayed, then go to: "Windows" → "Show View" → "Console"

To create a new Project, you will need to go to "File" → "New"→ "Java Project." This will open the "New Java Project" window. Here we can specify many things about the program we will be
creating. For now, just set the project name to "HelloWorld" then click "Finish." You should now see a small blue folder in the Package Explorer called "HelloWorld," this is our new project.

Next, right-click on the folder and select "New" → "Class." This will bring up the "New Java Class" window. This window will allow you to many of the settings that define a Java class. For right now we are only interested in two of these fields. First, set the "Name" of the class to "HelloWorld." Second click on the check box for "public static void main(String[] args)," this will create the Main Method in our program. Once you are done click "Finish."

Creating a Program In Intellij

After installing Intellij you will be ready to create your first program. To begin open Intellij and select "Create New Project" from the popup window. Once you do this the New Project Window will open.

When the next page loads check to see if Intellij has automatically found your Java SDK. If not, then you will have to click the "New..." button and select the SDK that you installed. Once your are done click next.

The next page allows you to load a project from a template. We won't be using any templates in this book so just make sure no templates are selected then click next.

The following page is were we define the name of our project . For this example change the project name to "HelloWorld" with no spaces. Once that is done select "Finish". At this point you might have to wait for Intellij to create your workspace. When it is done building a panel on the left hand side of the screen will appear with the name of our project "HelloWorld" and an arrow.

Select the arrow to expand our project folder. Right click on the "src" folder and select New → Java Class. Name the class "HelloWorld" and click "OK". This will load a new tab containing our code.

Now that you have successfully created your project, lets go over the different parts of the Intellij IDE.

- Active Tool Window: Located on the left-hand side of the screen, this is where we will see all of the files you are using in your current project.

- The Editor Window: The large blank space in the center of the screen is the editor window. This will be used later to edit and create our code.

- The Console: The console won't be visible until we run our code, but it will appear at the bottom of the screen. The console is where any print statements, errors, or other important information will be displayed when we run our programs.

Writing the Code

Now that you know what each part of the IDE does lets write the our first program. Change the code in the editor window to match the code bellow.

```
public class HelloWorld {

    public static void main (String [ ] args) {
            System.out.print( "Hello World!" );
    }

}
```

Now that you have created your code, you might be wondering what it does. We will walk through each and every part of the code explaining each piece.

- Class Definition: Tells Java what the class can and can't do (for right now we won't be adding any special restrictions to the class). It also tells us the name of our class (in this case "HelloWorld").

```
public class HelloWorld {

    public static void main (String [ ] args) {
            System.out.print( "Hello World!" );
    }

}
```

•Main Method: The first method that will be called when we run our program. You can think of this method as the boss that tells the program what to do.

```
public static void main (String [ ] args) {
    System.out.println( "Hello World!" );
}
```

•Open Brace({) : This tells Java where the class or method starts.

•Closing Brace(}) : This tells Java where the class ends or where the main method ends.

```
public class HelloWorld {

    public static void main (String [ ] args) {
        System.out.println( "Hello World!" );
    }

}
```

Now you might be wondering what the highlighted words mean. Some of these words are what we call a modifiers. Each modifier tells the compiler something about what the method, class, or variable can or cannot do. Here are two tables with some basic modifiers you might find useful, for a complete list of modifiers see "Useful Tables and References" in the back of this book.

Method Modifiers:

Modifier	Description
public	This class can be accessed by any other class
static	There can only be one method with this name in your program

Class Modifiers:

Modifier	Description
public	This class can be accessed by any other class
default	This class can only be used by other classes in the same package (folder).

Now let's take a closer look at the main method to see what it all means. We already know that public static means that the method can be accessed by any other class and that there can only be one main method in the program, but what does void mean? This part of the method signature is what we call the return type. You can think of a method as a machine that we can put stuff into (called the arguments or parameters) and we can sometimes get stuff back out (called the return type). In the case of our main method we don't want to return anything so we write void. The stuff in parentheses is the argument (the stuff me feed into the machine).

Every method you will ever create in Java will look like this:

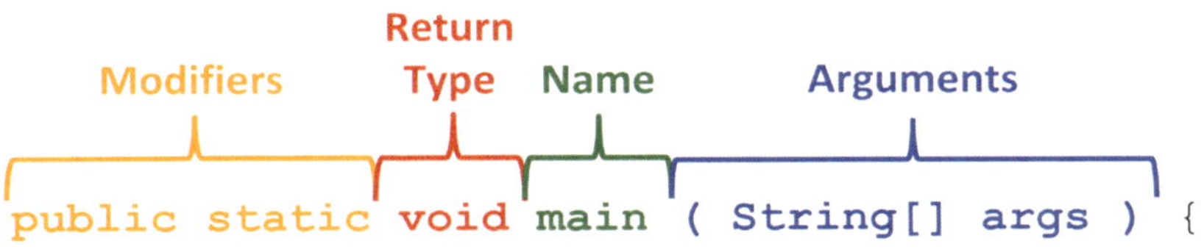

For right now don't worry too much about what the arguments portion of the method signature means, that will be discussed in a later chapter.

Depending on what IDE you chose you might also have an additional section of code that either begins with two forward slashes or is surrounded by "/*" and "*/". This is what is called a comment in Java. Anything written within the comment is ignored when you run the code. This feature can be used when you want to write about what certain sections of your code do. For more information on what you should comment see the style guide in the back of the book.

Next, lets talk about the print statement. Anything that is inside the two quotation marks will be printed to the console when the statement is ran.

```
public class HelloWorld {

    public static void main (String [ ] args) {
        System.out.println( "Hello World!" );
    }

}
```

To test the code, we need to compile and run it.

Eclipse Users:
Just click the green run button to launch the compiler. Eclipse may ask you to save you code at this point. If you have the console open, you should see *Hello World!* printed.

Intellij Users:
To run your code select Run > Run and a new dialogue window will open. From here select the code you want to run (thin this case select "HelloWorld". This will open the console and should print *Hello World!* in the console.

Congratulations! You have just created your first Java program! Although it may seem a little overwhelming right now, you have taken your first step into becoming a Java programmer.

Hello World - Exercises

1. What is the definition of a computer?

2. What are the two locations where memory is stored in a computer? What is each one used for?

3. What is machine language, and why would programmers not want to use it?

4. What is Java Byte code, and why is it used?

5. What are the three main editing windows in Eclipse?

6. A case sensitive language is a programming language that cares about capitalization (ex. "A" is different from "a"). Is Java a case sensitive language?

7. What are the two class modifiers, and what do they mean?

8. What are the five method modifiers and what do they mean?

9. What are the four parts of a method signature, and what does each one do?

10. Write a program that prints the following three lines in the console:

    Alpha
    Bravo
    Charlie

Chapter Two:
Variables

Imagine you have a standard deck of cards, where each of these cards have different suits with their corresponding values. Now you might be asking, what do these cards have to do with programming? Well, in programming, different values are stored within different suits, called variables. These variables can hold a variety of different values and types for as long as the type matches. An example of this would be say we picked up a card that was the 2 of Hearts. In this instance, the Hearts would be a data type (variable), and the 2 would be the data value stored in it. We achieve this through a process of instantiation.

Instantiation is the process that we use to create the variable. Each variable can only be instantiated once, and after that the values are free to do whatever you want them to.

An example of this if we used our card analogy would be:

```
Heart heart = 2
```

In code, it would look more like:

```
int heart = 2;
```

Notice that in front of the name that we gave, there lies the word *int* (in this case *int* is the data type). Overall there are many different data types that each hold their own respective variables. The different variables that we will be using throughout this book are int, double, boolean, char, and String.

What is an *int*?

An *int*, pronounced integer, is a type of variable that holds a specific type of number. The *int* data type can only hold whole numbers like -3, -2, -1, 0, 1, 2, 3. Integers can hold positive and negative values, and are often used for keeping a count of different objects and functions.

What is a *double*?

A *double* can be any number, including the ones with decimal points such as 1.2, 2.2 or 3.2. Although they can hold whole numbers like 1, 2, and 3, they are stored as 1.0, 2.0, 3.0. This is more useful for calculations and when you want to have a more precise value as an answer.

What is a *boolean*?

A *boolean* is a variable that can only hold true or false. This is important for telling your code to perform different functions or to change the output based on whether something is true or false. An example of this would be collision. Think of a video game that you have played. When you walk around, and say you walk into an object, do you run through it? Most likely not! This is because the code is telling the character that its movement is false when it collides, and therefore can't walk through the object. These types events will be discussed later in the book.

What is a *char*?

A *char*, short for character, is an individual character that has a specific ASCII (or numeric) value. Stored between single quotation marks such as *'a'*, chars are useful because they allow us to manipulate specific characters in words. An example of this would be an encryption program. This type of program would take in a bunch of different *chars*, and apply a change to each *char* so it could be stored as something else. Remember that is computer science a character can be anything from the a letter to a space (' '), period ('.'), or tab ('\t').

What is a *String*?

A *String* is defined as a character array, meaning that each *String* is full of multiple characters strung together to be stored in a single variable. Denoted by quotation marks (E.g. "Hello World"), *Strings* are useful because they hold words and phrases that can be printed out and used to display text, instead of having to print out each char individually. Also note that *Strings* use a capital "S". They are the only basic variable type that uses a capital letter.

Manipulation of Variables

Think back to the variable of *heart* that we created earlier. Now you might be thinking, what use is it is always 2 for its whole life? Well, it doesn't always have to be that way. There are various ways that you can change the variable so it holds other values, but keeps the same name. An example of this would be:

```
Heart heart = 2
heart = 3
heart = 4
```

Now what value does *heart* hold? 4. Also, notice how we did not have to declare what type *heart* was when we changed its value from 2 to 3 to finally 4. Another example would be:

```
int heart = 3;
heart += 1;
heart -= 2;
```

Now try and see what *heart* holds. If you guessed 2, then you guessed correctly! Don't worry if you didn't get the right answer. You may be asking yourself, what exactly does += and -= do? Take the example above. When we say that heart += 1, we are really saying:

```
heart = heart + 1;
```

However that can be shortened to using a += and the value we want to add to it after the symbols. Say we used:

```
heart += 1;
```

We would be adding 1 to heart due to the 1 being on the right side of the equation.

The same goes for -=. When we say -= 1, we are really saying:

```
heart = heart - 1;
```

The same holds true for using multiplication and division, denoted *= and /= respectively.

Modulus

You already know about addition, subtraction, multiplication, and division, but there is a fifth operator that you are probably not aware of. The modulus operator (represented by the percent sign %) is a mathematical operator used all the time in computer programing. Modulus returns the remainder after division of the two numbers given.

Now, that sounds super technical, so let's use the example of 5 % 2 (read 5 modulo 2). In order to do this, we divide 5 by 2 using long division.

1) How many 2s can we fit into 5 using only whole numbers?
   Answer: 2
2) Next, we multiply 2 by our answer.
   2 * 2 = 4
3) Then subtract the answer from 5.
   5 - 4 = 1
4) 1 is the remainder after division becasue two can't fit into 1.

This means that 5 % 2 = 1.

Variable Naming Conventions

An important rule to follow is that you can't name a variable whatever you want. There are many different names you can use however, as long as it follows these three rules:

1) Always start the name of the variable with a letter. This means that you can't start your variable with a number such as 2heart, but you can name the variable heart2.

2) Never put a space in your variable name. You must always remove all spaces.

3) Variable names and their cases are important. Hello is not the same variable as hello. Programmers also write using camel case, meaning that the first word is normally lower case and the following words are upper case, such as helloWorld (notice the w is capitalized).

4) Avoid underscores ("_") as much as possible

Variables - Exercises

1. What is a variable in Java?

2. Why are variables important to use when programming?

3. What do the following variable types store?
    a) double
    b) char
    c) boolean
    d) int
    e) String

4. What type of variable would be used for each of the following?
    a) -57
    b) a
    c) 0.258
    d) !
    e) Foxtrot

5. What does num += 1 do?

6. What does num /= 5 do?

7. What does the following code print?

```
double num = 0;
num += 10;
num /= 2;
num -= 3;
num += 1;
num *= num;
System.out.println( num );
```

8. What is the modulus operator?

9. Solve the following:
   a) 3 % 2
   b) 2 % 3
   c) 3 % 3
   d) 0 % 2
   e) 2 % 0

10. For each variable name state whether it should be renamed and why.
   a) num
   b) 97year
   c) GravityConstant
   d) primeNumber
   e) TEMP
   f) my_variable

Chapter Three:
Conditional Statements

Boolean Expressions

In the previous chapter, you learned about booleans and how they can hold values of either true or false. On their own booleans are not very useful. However, they can be used as a way of asking questions in a program when you combine them to form a boolean expression.

A boolean expression is a set of variables and operators that evaluates to either true or false. This is useful if you want to ask a question like is *num* an even number? This question can be coded into Java like this:

```
int num = 9;
boolean isEven = ((num % 2) == 0);
```

Remember that the modulus operator (%) returns the remainder of the first number divided by the second number. Any even number divided by 2 will always have a remainder of zero. Now you might have noticed that a double equals sign (==) was used instead of the usual single one (=). In short, == asks if something is equal to something else and = sets something equal to something else. The key point here is that == is a question and = is a statement.

Operator	Name	Description	Example
A == B	Equal To	Is A equal to B?	2 == 3 is *false*
A > B	Greater Than	Is A greater than B?	2 > 3 is *false*
A >= B	Greater Than or Equal To	Is A greater than or equal to B?	2 >= 3 is *false*
A < B	Less Than	Is A less than B?	2 < 3 is *true*
A <= B	Less Than or Equal to	Is A less than or equal to B?	2 <= 3 is *true*
A != B	Not Equal to	Is A not equal to B?	2 != 3 is *true*
!A	Not	Is the A false?	!false is *true*
A || B	Conditional Or	Is A and/or B true?	true || false is *true*
A && B	Conditional And	Are A and B both true?	true && false is *false*

You can also combine the logical operators to ask more complicated questions. For example, you could ask: (A > 5) && (A < 10). This is the same as saying "Is A greater than five and is A less than 10?"

The *If* Statement

Although we can now ask questions in our code we still can't change what the program does based on the answers to these questions. This is where the *if* statement comes in handy. An *if* statement is a form of selection that tells our code to do something different depending on the answer to the question. For example, here is a code that prints out "Is Even" only is num is even.

```
int num = 9;
if ( ( num % 2 ) == 0 ) {
    System.out.println( "Is Even" );
}
```

Notice that we surround the code in the code in the *if* statement with curly braces ({ }), just like with methods and classes.

In addition to the *if* statement you can add an *else* statement. The *else* will catch anything that doesn't correctly answer the question in the original *if* statement. We can add this into our previous code to tell if a number is odd. The following code will print out “Is Even” for even numbers, and “Is Odd” for any number that is not even.

```
int num = 9;
if ( ( num % 2 ) == 0 ) {
    System.out.println( "Is Even" );
} else {
    System.out.println( "Is Odd" );
}
```

In English, the code above reads: If num is even, print “Is Even,” else, print “Is Odd.”

You can also expand the *if* statement to include an *else if.* The code bellow would read: If num is even print “Is Even,” else if num is negative print “Is Negative Odd, otherwise print “Is Positive Odd.” Remember that only one selection statement can be chosen per *if* statement.

```
int num = 9;
if ( ( num % 2 ) == 0 ) {
    System.out.println( "Is Even" );
} else if (num < 0) {
    System.out.println( "Is Negative Odd" );
} else {
    System.out.println( "Is Positive Odd" );
}
```

Ternary Operators

Although *if* statements can be very useful, it can sometimes be a pain to write out an entire *if* statement for something very simple. For cases like this we use a short hand version called the ternary operator. A ternary operator can be thought of as a one line *if/else* statement.

Ternary operators are typically only used when assigning a value to a variable, as longer statements can be hard to read.

For example the following code assigns the value *2* to the variable *a* if num is positive. Otherwise it assigns the value of *40* to *a*.

```
int num = 9;
int a = num > 0 ? 2 : 40
```

In general any ternary operator is structured like this:

variable* = *boolean statement* ? *value if true* : *value if false

A few rules for using ternary operators:

1.) Only use them for short boolean expressions
2.) Do NOT nest ternary operators. This makes them almost impossible to read.
3.) If something will require more than one ternary operator use an *if* statement instead.

Conditional Statements - Exercises

1. What is a boolean expression?

2. Why are boolean expressions useful when coding?

3. Evaluate the following boolean expressions:
    a) ! (false)
    b) true && true
    c) false || false
    d) ! (false && true) || false

4. Evaluate the following boolean expressions:
    a) 5 > 0
    b) 6 != (24 / 3)
    c) (3 != 5) && (4 > 6)
    d) (10 % 6 <= 2) || ((5 * 4 == 20) && ! (8 == 7 + 3))

5. To determine if a number is even we could use (num % 2) == 0.
   What would we use to tell if a number is a multiple of 17?

6. Exclusive Or (xor) is an additional boolean operator.
   It is defined like this:

   ! (A && B) && (A || B)

   Describe what xor does.

7. What will the following code print?

```
int num = 26;

if ( num < 20 ) {
    System.out.println ( "Less than 20" );
} else if ( num  % 2 == 0 ) {
    System.out.println ( "Even" );
} else if ( num > 0 ) {
    System.out.println ( "Greater than 0" );
} else {
    System.out.println( num );
}
```

8. What does the following code print?

```
int num = 125;

int a = num >= 0 ? 1, -1;
int b = a + num == 124 ? 60 : 50;
char c = (a + b) / num > 10 ? 'x' : 'z';

System.out.println( a );
System.out.println( b );
System.out.println( c );
```

Chapter Four:

Loops

Why are they important?

Imagine that you had been tasked with adding up all the numbers between zero and ten. This wouldn't take too long to do by hand and it would be simple program. But what if you had been asked to add all the numbers up to 1,000? 100,000,000? At this point it would no longer be practical to add these numbers by hand or to write each addition as its own line of code. However, by using loops we can get this task done easily. A loop is a section of code that is done repeatedly until a certain condition is met.

While Loops:

The *while* loop is the most basic of the loops but also the most powerful. At the top of the while loop you have a condition. This condition is always a boolean expression and the loop will continue to run until the expression is false. Inside the loop we put the code we want to run repeatedly. Below is a while loop that adds all the numbers between zero and one thousand.

```
int num = 1;   // The number to be added
int sum = 0;   // The current sum

while ( num <= 1000 ) {
    sum += num;
    num++;
}

System.out.println( sum );
```

In this example the while loop will run as long as *num* is <= 1000. Each time the loop is run *num* will be added to the sum variable. Then, *num* will be incremented by 1 (this is what *num++* means).

When *num* reaches the value 1001, it will no longer be <= 1000. So, when we ask our question again it will be false. This means that we can exit our loop, going to the *System.out.println(sum).*

The most important thing to remember when creating loops is to make sure that it will end at some point. A loop that never ends is called an infinite loop, and can be very dangerous in more complicated programs because they can cause strange and unpredictable things to happen. A simple example would be to change the increment (*num++*) to a decrement (*num*--). In this case *num* will always be less than on thousand so the loop will never exit. Before you run any program will a loop in it double check that no infinite loops exist.

For Loops:

The second type of loop is called a *for* loop. These loops specialize in changing a variable until its value reaches a certain number. Here is the same code that calculates the sum of all numbers from zero to one thousand using a *for* loop.

```
int sum = 0;   // The current sum

for ( int num = 0; num <= 1000; num++ ) {
    sum += num;
}

System.out.print( sum );
```

Let's break down the loop. The first part of the loop creates a new integer variable called *num* and sets it equal to zero. The second part tells us that loop will end when *num* is no longer less than or equal to 1000. Lastly, the third part tells us that after each time the loop is run we will increment *num* by one.

So, the first time we enter the for loop sum is equal to zero and num is equal to zero. We check if *num* is <= 1000. It is so we enter the for loop. Next, we add *num* to sum (0 = 0 + 0) so sum is still zero. When we reach the ending brace ('}') we add one to *num* because the last part of the *for* loop says *num++*. So, *num* is now equal to one.

Then we loop back up to the top of the *for* loop and ask our question again: is *num <= 1000*? Yes, so we enter the *for* loop again. This time when we compute *sum += num* we will get 1 = 0 + 1. Once again when we reach the closing brace of our *for* loop we add one to *num*.

This will continue until our question is no longer true (*num* is no longer less than or equal to 1000). When this happens we exit our *for* loop. This simply means that we skip all the way to the code after our closing brace. In this example, when we exit our *for* loop we would go right to the *System.out.println(sum);*

So far we have only talked about *num++* and *num--*, but there is also *++num* and *–num*. When the ++ or - - is placed before the variable in a *for* loop, the increment or decrement is evaluated before we ask our question. This means that is we used ++num in the above example: num would start at 0, then be incremented to 1, then num (1) would be added to sum.

Although an increment or decrement is often used in a *for* loop, you don't have to do that. The following program adds all the powers of two between one and one thousand.

```
int sum = 0;   // The current sum
for ( int i = 0; i <= 1000; i *= 2 ) {
    sum += i;
}

System.out.print( sum );
```

As you can probably see, a *for* loop is just a fancy while loop. As a programmer, it is good practice to use a *for* loop whenever you can because they are often easier to read and understand than *while* loops. However, *while* loops can be much more powerful than *for* loops in certain situations.

Do While Loops:

The *do while* loop is probably the hardest loop to understand. Much like a *while* loop, the *do while* loop has one boolean expression that it checks every time it loops. If this expression is false it stops looping and exits.

However, unlike a *while* loop we ask this question at the end of the loop (not at the beginning). This means that a *do while* loop will always execute at least once. An example *do while* loop that calculates the sum of all numbers from one to one thousand is shown below.

```
int sum = 0;   // The current sum
int num = 0;
do {
    num++;
    sum += num;
} while ( num < 1000 );

System.out.print( sum );
```

Note that because we ask our question at the end (after we add one to *num*) we have to change our question to ask if *num < 1000* rather than *num <= 1000*. We do this because when *num* is equal to 999 (less than 1000) we know that we will add one to it after immediately after we ask our question (adding 1000 to our sum). However, when *num* is equal to 1000 if we let it loop again it would actually add 1001 to our sum (something we don't want).

In practice you shouldn't use a *do while* loop unless it makes the program significantly easier to understand, shorter, or more efficient. For a beginner you should try sticking to *for* and *while* loops whenever possible.

Loops - Exercises

1. What is a loop and why are they useful?

2. What is a while loop?

3. What is an infinite loop and why are they dangerous?

4. What is a for loop?

5. What does the following code print?

```
int num = 100;

while ( num > 0 ) {
    System.out.println( num );
    num -= 20;
}
```

6. What does the following code print?

```
int sum = 0;

for ( int i = 2; i < 50; i += 1 ) {
    if ( i % 2 == 0 ) {
          sum += i;
    }
}
```

7. What is a do while loop?

8. Write a program that adds all of the even numbers between 2 and 50.

9. What do num++ and ++num do?

Chapter Five:

Arrays

Suppose you wanted to have a program that stores the grades of all one hundred students in a programing class. Although we could create one hundred variables to hold every person's grade this would take a lot of time and make our code hard to read. Thankfully programmers have created a way to do exactly that in a simple and easy to understand way.

An array is a chunk of computer memory that is reserved for a certain type of variable. These chunks can hold as few as one variable or as many as the computer allows (many, many more than we will ever need in this book). All the variables stored in this way are assigned a unique number so that you can pull them out of memory whenever you need to. For example, the array bellow hold up to eight variables (x) numbered 0-7.

0	1	2	3	4	5	6	7
X_1	X_2	X_3	X_4	X_5	X_6	X_7	X_8

Always remember that the numbering (called indexing) of the array starts at zero. So, the fifth element in the array is indexed as 4.

To create an array in Java we first need to specify what type of variable we are saving in our chunk of memory. We then need to name the array and specify how many elements it can hold. The size of an array cannot be changed once it is created, so it is important to use the correct size in the beginning. Below are the three different ways to create an array in Java.

1) int [ ] exampleOne = new int [5];
   - Creates an empty array that can hold up to 5 integers

2) int [ ] exampleTwo = new int [ ] { -2, -1, 0, 1, 2 }
   - Creates an array that holds 1, 2, 3, 4, and 5

3) int [ ] exampleThree = { -2, -1, 0, 1, 2 }
   - Creates an array that holds 1, 2, 3, 4, and 5

In all the cases above the size of the array is set to five. In the first example this is easy to see, but in the lower two the size is equal to the number of elements that we initialize the array with. To access an element in any of the 3 arrays, you would just write exampleThree[2], which returns 0.

For example, the code bellow creates an array then prints the element at index 2 in the array 'c'.

```
char [ ] letters = { 'a', 'b', 'c', 'd', 'e' };

System.out.println( letters[ 2 ] );
```

If we wanted to print all the elements in an array we could make a print statement for each element, but because we know how to use For loops we can make this much simpler.

```
char [ ] alpha = { 'a', 'b', 'c', 'd', 'e' };

for ( int i = 0; i < alpha.length - 1; i++ ) {
    System.out.print( alpha[ i ] );
}
```

This code will print each letter in the array starting with index 0 and up to the last index in the array. The "alpha.length" gives us the number of elements in the alpha array.

Since the last index of any array is always equal to the size of the array minus one, we can tell our For loop to keep looping while i <= alpha.length – 1. However, (i <= alpha.length – 1) is equivalent to saying (i < alpha.length), so either one can be used but most programmer us (i < alpha.length) because it is much shorter to type an looks cleaner.

But what happens if we try to get an element that isn't in our array? What if we asked Java to give us the element at -1 or 3,000? In both cases Java would throw an exception and end (or terminate) your program once it has reached that line of code. To be more specific, whenever you try to reach an index that doesn't exist. This is called trying to access an index that is "out of bounds."

Adding in what we learned from the last chapter we can create the following program that separates an array of even and odd integers into separate arrays by using a for loop and an if statement. Now we will walk through the program step by step. First we initialized our variables we would need. Then, we created a For loop that starts at i = 0 and continues as long as i is less than the length (or size) of the array. We then check if the number is even or odd, and add it to the correct array.

```
int [ ] n = { 1, 2, 3, 4, 5, 6, 7, 8, 9, 10 };
int [ ] even = new int [ 5 ];
int evenIndex = 0;
int [ ] odd = new int [ 5 ];
int oddIndex = 0;

for ( int i = 0; i < n.length; i++ ) {
    if ( ( n[ i ] % 2 ) == 0 ) {
          even [ evenIndex ] n [ i ];
          evenIndex++;
    } else {
          odd [ oddIndex ] = numbers [ i ];
          oddIndx++;
    }
}
```

Arrays - Exercises

1. What is an array?

2. How are arrays useful? When should we use arrays rather than normal variables?

3. What number does Java begin indexing at?

4. For each of the following, create an array that holds the stated values.

    a) An array of 5 integers
    b) An array of 60 characters
    c) An array that holds: Alpha, Beta, Gama, Delta
    d) An array that holds: 0.1, 2.25, -89, 1534.15

5. What does the following program print?

```
int [ ] z = { 100, 34, 40, 17, 392, 87 };
int [ ] m = { 1, 2, 3, 4, 5, 6};

int zlength = z.length;
int mlength = m.length;

for ( int i = 0; i < zlength; i++ ) {
    if ( (mlength + i ) % 4 > 3 ) {
          z [ i ] = m [ i ] * 4;
    } else {
          z [ i ] = z [ i ] * m [ i ];
    }
}

System.out.println(Arrays.toString(z));
```

Chapter Six:
Strings

One type of variable you might still have questions is the String. As you already know, a String a variable that contains a series of letters and symbols. A simple example of a string would be "Hello World!!!" You might also remember that a char is a variable that holds a single letter or symbol, for example 'a'. What you might not know is that a String is just a special type of array that holds chars.

The String "Hello!!!" can be thought of as the following array, where each character is one element in the array.

0	1	2	3	4	5	6	7
H	e	l	l	o	!	!	!

However, there are a few differences between Strings and Arrays that you should know about:

	char [ ] word = {'h', 'i' }	String word = "hi
Get a Letter	word [0]	word.charAt(0)
Change a Letter	word [1] = 'Z'	Must create a new String: word = "hZ"
Print	Must convert to a String before printing: String(word)	Use normal printing conventions
Get Size	word.length	word.length()
Adding New Elements	A new array must be created char[] wordTwo = {'h', 'i', '!'}	word += "!"

By far the two biggest differences to keep in mind is that an array can be changed but a String cannot, and that you can always make a String longer but an array has a fixed length.

Here are two example codes, one uses a String the other uses an array. Both codes do the same thing.

String:

```
String word = "Fox"

if ( word.charAt( 2 ) == 'x' ) {
    word += "trot";
}

System.out.println( word );
```

Array:

```
char [ ] word = { 'F', 'o', 'x' };

if ( word [ 2 ] == 'x' ) {
    word = new char [ ] {'F', 'o', 'x', 't',
          'r', 'o', 't' };
}

System.out.println( Arrays.toString( word ) );
```

Another useful method is the toCharArray ( )
This method takes a String, and turns it into a character array. This makes it useful for manipulation of the different characters, and you can always turn it back into a String later.

The following code uses this method to change the String to a char array, and then back to a String.

```
String word = "Fox";

char [ ] cw = word.toCharArray( );

String result = new String(cw);
```

Other useful tricks that one can use to manipulate strings are the toUpperCase( ) and toLowerCase( ) methods. These methods are incredibly useful for when trying to make a String all the same case, eliminating the need for case sensitivity.

The code below prints out "HELLO" and "hello" respectively

```
String word = "Fox";

word = word.toUpperCase( );
System.out.println( word );

word = word.toLowerCase( );
System.out.println( word );
```

Special Characters

When printing Strings there are a few things that you might want to print but don't know how to. For example, how do you print a tab, go to a new line, or print a quotation mark?

To add any of these to our Strings we need the backslash character "\". The when Java sees the backslash in a String or char it lets Java know that it needs to print something special. Below are the codes for a few different characters you might find useful. Experiment with them to see what they look like when printed.

Special Charcter	What is Printed
\"	Double Quotation Mark
\'	Single Quotation Mark
\\	Back Slash
\n	New Line
\t	Tab
\b	Backspace
\r	Carriage Return

Comparing Two Strings

If you want to compare two Strings to see if they are equal you can't just use the normal equality operator ("=="). Instead you will have to use a special equals methods. (Methods will be discussed in greater detail in the next chapter).

Here is an example code that compares two strings to see if they are the same.

```
String strA = "cat";
String strB = "CAT";

if ( strA.equals( strB ) ) {
    System.out.println( "Equal" );
} else {
    System.out.println( "Not Equal" );
}
```

In this example the code will print "Not Equal". Remember that Java is case sensitive. This means that "cat" does not equal "CAT".

Strings - Exercises

1. What is a String?

2. Why would Java have a specific variable for char arrays but no others?

3. Convert the following strings to char arrays, give the index for each letter.
   a) "Hi"
   b) "abcdefghijk"
   c) "To be or not 2 be?"

4. For each of the following operations, say whether Strings and/or char arrays can perform that operation.
   a) Change a character
   b) Print
   c) Get a letter at a specific position
   d) Add a new letter

5. What does the following code print?

```
String str = "Today is ";
String str2 = "sunny";
String str3 = "clOUdy";

if ( str.length >= 5 ) {
    str = str.toUpperCase( );
    str += str2.toLowerCase( );
} else {
    str = str.toLowerCase( );
    str += str3.toUpperCase( );
}
System.out.println( str );
```

6. What is the importance of the toCharArray( ) method?

Chapter Seven:
Methods

Basic Methods

As you start to put together all of the different things that you have learned, you might begin to notice that your code is getting rather complicated and crowded. A way that programmers deal with this, and to keep their code more organized and efficient, is to use different methods.

Methods are created much like a class, however with fewer identifying keywords. An example of a method would be:

```
public String getTheString ( String x ) {
    // your code here
    return x;
}
```

If we take a closer look at each of the words that make up the declaration of the method, we see the words public, String, getTheString, and (String x). Each of these means something, and can be changed.

Public is the visibility declaration of the method. Public means that anyone can use this method. Private on the other hand means means that only this class can use it.

(See *Useful Tables and Reference* for a list of modifiers)

String, the second word, is the return type. In this example, the method would return a String variable. However, if the second word was int, the method would have to return an integer.

The third word "getTheString" is the name of the method. Every method should be named using conventional rules: the first word is lowercase, and all following words are uppercase.

(String x) is the input for the method. When calling upon the method, you must put in your inputs, so that the method can have access to the data. An example of this would be:

```
getTheString ( "hi" );
```

This code would set the input variable x to equal "hi". The line return x; inside of our method gives the variable after the return keyword (in this case x) to whatever is calling the method.

Not all methods have to return something. Some methods are created to set values to different variables, and to perform different tasks. In order to show that a method doesn't return anything, we use the keyword void instead of a return type. An example of this would be:

```
String g = "";

public void setTheString ( String x ) {
    g = x;
}
```

The code above creates a string that the rest of the class can use. This is useful so that many other methods can use the same String, instead of it not having a consistent value throughout your code. Also, notice how the return type is replaces by the word void, and therefore the method has no return statement.

A good rule of thumb to follow is: methods should only perform one overall task. This is to keep it from getting over crowded, and to make sure that the inputs match up. While that might seem a nuisance, it is important to remember that you can have as many methods as you want, and that there is no limit to the amount of inputs that a method can take in. As for return types, you can return any type of variable, array, object, etc. so long as you only return one thing.

Recursion

Another useful trick in programming is the art of mastering recursion. Recursion is any action that occurs when a method calls upon itself multiple times. This can be a real challenge to sometimes because of the threat of creating infinite loops. However, with the basics of if statements and other conditionals, simple recursion is an easy feat to accomplish.

In the following example, we use a for loop to add all numbers less than a given number n.

```
public int sum ( int n ) {
    int sum = 0;

    for ( int i = n; i > 0; i-- ) {
            sum += i;
    }

    return sum;
}
```

The code can be rewritten recursively as follows:

```
public int sumR ( int n ) {

    if ( n < = 1 ) {
            return 1;
    } else {
            return n + sumR ( n - 1 );
    }

}
```

The first *if* statement is called the base case. The base case is the most important part of any recursive code. If it is defined incorrectly or doesn't exist at all, the program can enter infinite recursion. This can cause our program to crash, freeze, or otherwise behave unpredictably. In the example on the previous page, any number passed to our method will eventually reach a value that is less than or equal to 1. This is guaranteed because we are always subtracting.

A more complex example of recursion is used to calculate the Fibonacci numbers. In case you don't know what they are, the Fibonacci numbers are a famous set of numbers where the next number in the series is equal to the sum of the previous two numbers. The sequence starts with 0, 1, 1, 2, 3, 5, 8, and so on.

As you can see 1 = 1 + 0, 2 = 1 + 1, 3 = 2 + 1. . . Here is the code to calculate these numbers using recursion.

```
public int fib ( int n ) {

    if ( n == 0 ) {
         return 0;
    } else if ( n == 1 ) {
         return 1;
    } else {
         return fib( n - 1 ) + fib ( n - 2 );
    }

}
```

This code returns the n'th Fibonacci number (ex. fib(4) returns 3). In this case, we have two base cases (n == 1 and n==0). We need both because our recursive program calls n – 1 and n – 2.

Methods - Exercises

1. What is a method?

2. What do each of the following methods return?

    a) public String printHello (int g) {
    b) public double [ ] getTaxInfo (String name) {
    c) public void calculatePosition (char alpha, char beta) {

3. What is the input of each of these methods?

    a) public boolean isAtHome (int houseNumber) {
    b) public void printInfo (String department) {
    c) public double [ ] makeGrid (String name, int x, int y) {

4. How many methods can be put in each Java program?

5. Why are methods helpful?

6. What does the return keyword do in Java?

7. What does the following code print?

```
public class Example {

  public int getInteger ( int i ) {
        return i * 2;
  }

  public static void main ( String args [ ] ) {
        int i = 5;
        int j = getInteger ( i );
        System.out.println ( j );
  }
}
```

8. Will the following code run? If not, explain the error in the code and how to fix it.

```
public class Example {

  public int getInteger ( int a, int b ) {
         return ( a * b ) + a;
  }

  public static void main ( String args [ ] ) {

         int a = 5;
         int c = getInteger ( a );
         System.out.println ( c );

  }
}
```

9. Will the following code run? If not, explain the error in the code and how to fix it.

```
public class Example {

  public int getS ( String name, int a ) {
         String result = "Happy Birthday ";
         String result += name;
         return a;
  }

  public static void main ( String args [ ] ) {

         String jon = "Jon";
         String message = getS ( jon, 13 );
         System.out.println( message );

  }
}
```

10. What is recursion and why is it a useful tool?

11. What are the dangers to recursion?

12. What does the following recursive program print?

```
public class Example {

  public int getNumber ( int n ) {

        if ( n <= 0 ) {
             return 1;
        } else {
             return ( n * getNumber ( n - 1 );
        }

  }

  public static void main ( String args [ ] ) {

        int number = getNumber ( 4 );
        System.out.println ( number );

  }
}
```

Chapter Eight: Objects

Basic Objects

Up to this point everything you have coded in Java has been in one class file. We are now going to be creating other class files to use in our programs. This will allow us to create more complex programs and to make our programs much easier to read. However, to understand what it means to use multiple classes we must first go over something called an object. In Java you can think of an object and a class as the same thing (although this isn't exactly true in all fields of computer programming).

In Java an object is anything that you can describe. That might sound very vague, but an object can be literally anything that can be described using numbers, words, actions, etc. For example, we can describe a lion using a table. We call tables like this UML (Unified Modeling Language) diagrams. They are very useful for explaining what an object is and what it can do. By looking at our UML diagram of a lion we can easily see what things need to be included in our object.

Lion	← **Name**
- Has Fur - Has Claws - Has a Tail - Lives in the Savana - Age - Weight	← **Characteristics**
- Eat - Sleep - Pounce - Roar	← **What It Can Do (Actions)**

We are now going to create our lion object. So, lets create a new project called "Zoo" and a new class also called "Zoo." (Remember to create your main method in this Zoo class.) To create our lion, add a new class to the project by right-clicking on our Zoo Class and selecting New → Class. Name this class "Lion." Do not make a main method in this class, we don't want to have two main methods in our project.

You should now see a new class in the source folder named "Lion". In Java you can created as many classes are you need for your program. However, it is always good practice to use packages (folders) to organize class files when you start getting too many of them. Typically once you have six or more class files you should start thinking about placing them in packages. For this program we won't be needing packages.

Right now, our Lion object doesn't do anything. To fix this, add the list of characteristics to the Lion class as variables.

```
public class Lion {

    boolean hasFur = true;
    boolean hasClaws = true;
    boolean hasTail = true;

    String habitat = "Savana";

    int age = 0;
    int weight = 300;

}
```

Our object now has descriptions of what it is, but it still can't "do" anything. Let's add some methods to our *Lion* describing things it can "do".

```
public class Lion {

    //----------Characteristics----------------
    boolean hasFur = true;
    boolean hasClaws = true;
    boolean hasTail = true;

    String habitat = "Savana";

    int age = 0;
    int weight = 300;

    //----------------Actions------------------

    public String eat ( String food ) {
         return "Ate: " + food;
    }

    public String sleep ( ) {
         return "zzzzzz";
    }

    public String pounce ( String animal ) {
         return "Pounced on: " + animal;
    }

    public String roar ( ) {
         return "ROAAAAAAAAAAAR!!!";
    }

}
```

Our object now has variables that define it and methods that tell us what it can do, but if we run our program it doesn't do anything. The reason nothing happens is we have not instantiated (loaded) our Lion in our main method. To do this switch back to the *Zoo* class. Change the main method to look like this:

```
public static void main ( String [ ] args ) {

    Lion simba = new Lion ( );

}
```

Accessibility

We have now created a new *Lion* object called "simba." In Java, classes like *Lion* always begin with a uppercase letter, but the names of specific objects like *simba* begin with a lowercase letter.

Although we now have a Lion named *simba* in our *Zoo* class, it still doesn't do anything. Like with all programing we must tell our program what to do with this new object. Let's access a few of its variables and print them out:

```
public static void main ( String [ ] args ) {

    Lion simba = new Lion ( );

    boolean hasClaws = simba.hasClaws;
    String habitat = simba.habitat;
    int age = simba.age;

    System.out.println ( hasClaws );
    System.out.println ( habitat );
    System.out.println ( age );

}
```

The code above outputs:

true
Savana
8

As can be seen in the above example, we can easily access the variables from the objects we create. To do this we simply write the name of our object (*simba*), then add what is called a "dot operator" (it's just a period but programmers like to be fancy), followed by the variable we want to access. For exam if we wanted to access *simba's* weight we would write: simba.weight

simba	.	weight
Name of Object	Dot Operator	Name of Variable We Want

To use one of our methods in Lion we do something very similar:

simba	.	roar ( )
Name of Object	Dot Operator	Name of Method We Want

So, if we wanted to make our Lion roar we could write:

```
public static void main ( String [ ] args ) {

    Lion simba = new Lion ( );
    System.out.println ( simba.roar ( ) );

}
```

The code above prints "ROAAAAAAAAAAAR!!!"

Earlier in this book we talked about the difference between methods and variables that are declared *public* vs *private*. Although it probably didn't seem very important back then, this is where it makes a big difference. Anything that is declared public can be accessed using the dot operator. Whereas anything declared private can't be used with the dot operator.

For example, if we changed the roar method in *Lion* to private Eclipse would give us an error saying that it doesn't have permission to use *roar( )* in our main method. By default, every variable in Java is public unless you tell it not to be.

By using these public/private modifies we can create variables and methods that can only be used by the object that they are located in. These private methods and variables are often used for security reasons. Because no one can access these variables/methods they can't be tampered with by buggy or malicious programs.

Constructors

We now have one *Lion* in our *Zoo*, but what if we wanted to add three *Lions*? One hundred? Of course, these *Lions* are not going to have the same weight or age, and it would be a nightmare trying to write a class of each *Lion*. This is where constructors come in handy. A constructor is a simple section of code that acts like a method. Its one and only job is to load initial values into our object, and to help with the instantiation process.

Basic Constructor Example:

```
public NameOfClass ( input1, input2, ... ) {

    //What we do with the inputs:
    .
    .
    .

}
```

Before we can add a constructor to our Lion class we will need to make a few small changes first. Because we are initializing (setting) some of the variables when we make the class, we no longer have to define these variables explicitly. Secondly, when we create our *Lion* in the *Zoo* we must tell our *Lion* what the value of these variables are.

```
public class Lion {
    .
    .
    .
    int age;
    int weight;

    public Lion ( int age, int weight ) {
        this.age = age;
        this.weight = weight;
    }
    .
    .
    .
}
```

If you look at the constructor in our *Lion* class you will see that we are taking in an integer for the age of our *Lion* and another integer for the *Lion's* weight. The next line states: this.age = age; What does that mean? In Java the keyword "this" refers to the object you are currently inside of (in this case "this" refers to the *Lion* object). Therefor you could read the lines as "This object's age is equal to the input age." If you don't want to use the "this" keyword, all you must do is name the input variable something different form other variable in your class:

```
    .
    .
    .
    public Lion ( int newAge, int newWeight ) {
        age = newAge;
        weight = newWeight;
    }
    .
    .
    .
```

If we now look at our *Zoo* class, you will see that we now have an error. Because we created a constructor that takes in two integers for age and weight, we need to add these values when we create a *Lion*.

```
public static void main ( String [ ] args ) {

    Lion simba = new Lion ( 8, 300 );

}
```

Now that we have a way to create multiple *Lions* efficiently . Why don't we make an array of them? In this example we create an array of 50 Lions. Then, using a for loop we are able to initialize each lion with an age equal to *i* and a weight equal to *i**30*.

```
public static void main ( String [ ] args ) {

    Lion [ ] pride = new Lion [ 50 ];

    for ( int i = 0; i < pride.length; i++ ) {
        pride [ i ] = new Lion (i, i * 30 );
    }

}
```

Notice that we don't have to name each object. For all practical purposes none of these *Lions* have a "name," they are just members in an array.

Inheritance

What if we wanted to add a *Tiger* to our *Zoo*? A basic UML diagram for a *Tiger* can be seen in below. According to our UML diagram the only difference between a *Lion* and a *Tiger* is one has stripes and they live in different places. Although our *Lion* class is small enough that rewriting it wouldn't be too terrible, imagine what it would be like if the class was hundreds of lines long? We wouldn't want to rewrite the entire code just to change and/or add one variable. To fix this issue we use something called inheritance. Before we can do that though, we must first determine which object is the parent and which is the child.

Lion
- Has Fur - Has Claws - Has a Tail - **Lives in the Savana** - Age - Weight
- Eat - Sleep - Pounce - Roar

Tiger
- Has Fur - Has Claws - Has a Tail - **Lives in the Jungle** - **Has Stripes** - Age - Weight
- Eat - Sleep - Pounce - Roar

Determining Inheritance:

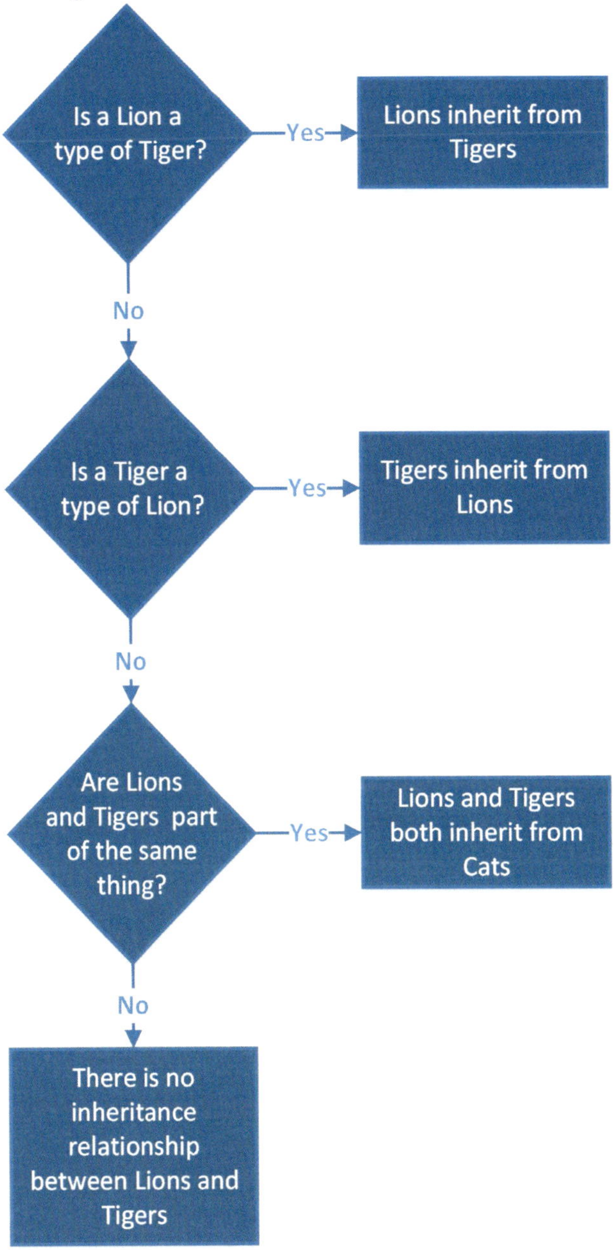

By using this diagram we can determine that *Tigers* and *Lions* inherit from *Cats*.

When we say, "Tigers inherit from Cats" what we mean is everything that describes a *Cat* also describes a *Tiger*, but what describes a *Tiger* doesn't always describe a basic *Cat*. We represent this relationship in our UML diagram like this:

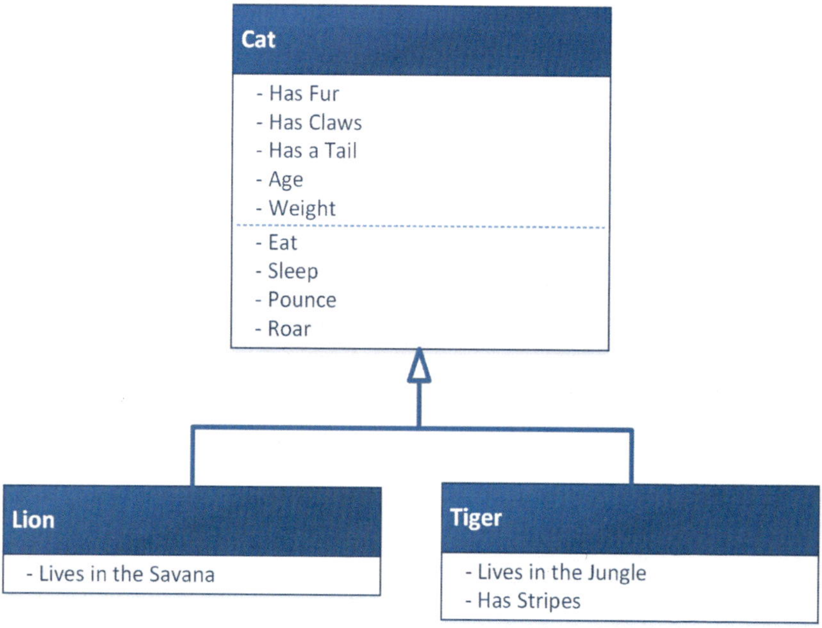

In this version of the UML diagram the arrows show an inheritance relationship. It is also important to remember that this arrow head is a triangle that is not filled in with a solid line. Although they won't be discussed in this book, there are other types of arrows that mean completely different things. So be sure to only use this type of arrow when showing inheritance. Additionally, in each child Object (*Tiger* and *Lion*) we only write the changes from the parent object (*Cat*). For Example, because the *Cat* object has a tail we don't have to define that in the *Lion* or *Tiger* objects.

Here is the code updated code to include the inheritance relationship.

```
public class Cat {

    //------------Characteristics----------------
    boolean hasFur = true;
    boolean hasClaws = true;
    boolean hasTail = true;

    String habitat = "Earth";

    int age;
    int weight;

    //------------Constructor------------------
    public Cat ( int age, int weight ) {

        this.age = age;
        this.weight = weight;

    }

    //------------Actions------------------------
    public String eat ( String food ) {
        return "Ate: " + food;
    }

    public String sleep ( ) {
        return "zzzzzz";
    }

    public String pounce ( String animal ) {
        return "Pounced on: " + animal;
    }

    public String roar ( ) {
        return "ROAAAAAAR!!!!";
    }

}
```

```
public class Lion extends Cat {

    String habitat = "Savana";

    public Lion ( int age, int weight ) {
          super ( age, weight );
    }

}
```

```
public class Tiger extends Cat {

    String habitat = "Savana";
    boolean hasStripes = true;

    public Tiger ( int age, int weight ) {
          super ( age, weight );
    }

}
```

At the beginning of each of the two child objects we tell Java that the object "extends" a parent. This is the inheritance relationship that we have been talking about, "extends" is just another word for "inherits from." Secondly, notice that the constructors in both *Tiger* and *Lion* call "super(age, weight)." In Java the keyword "super" means "Get this from my parent." In other words, the constructors in the *Lion* and *Tiger* classes are telling Java to use their parent's constructor. This is a simple way to avoid having to rewrite a constructor multiple times.

Overriding Methods:

Lastly, what would we do if we wanted to change a method defined in a parent object? For example, what if we wanted to change the roar method in the *Tiger* class to say something different. To do this we must override the parent class's method, by adding the override annotation. An annotation a simple line of text in a program that tells the Java interpreter some extra information about the program.

To change the roar method in the *Tiger* just add this to the class.

```
@Override
public String roar ( ) {
    return "Grrrrrrr";
}
```

Abstract VS Final:

There are two modifiers that define how we inherit methods, classes, and variables.

Variables:

- **final**: Marking a variable final means that its value can never be changed, even if it is inherited. You should use this to define constants in your program.

Methods:

- **abstract**: Making a method abstract means that the method must be overwritten by a child. (You <u>cannot</u> use the parent's method.) This is used if you don't know how the child will behave. Also know that when you declare an abstract method you don't implement the method's body.

```
public abstract int example( int a, int b );
```

- **final**: Making a method final means that it can't be overwritten by any of its children. This is typical used for security reasons or to force all children behave a certain way.

Classes:

- **abstract**: Marking a class as abstract means the class can't be used to make an object. Only the class's children can be used. Use this if you want to define a basic "blueprint" for a child.

Objects - Exercises

1. What is an object?

2. What is a UML diagram?

3. Using what you know about UML diagrams, create a UML diagram that describes your room.

4. Using your diagram from question 3, show an inheritance relationship between your room, the living room, and your house.

5. What type of arrow symbolizes inheritance in a UML diagram?

6. Describe what the @Override annotation does

7. Describe what the extends keyword does.

8. How many classes can you extend at once?

9. Describe what the dot operator (.) does.

10. Using the UML diagram showing the inheritance relationship in this chapter, add the following animals to the diagram: Polar Bear, Penguin, Clam

11. What is a constructor?

12. In Java, a class can have more than one constructor (so long as they have different inputs). Why might this be useful?

Chapter Nine:

Object Structures

Advanced Object Design

In the last chapter, you were introduced to basic object oriented design. This included how to create a basic object and the fundamentals of inheritance. However, objects are even more powerful than anything we discussed in the previous chapter. One of the most important tools in advanced object design is pointers.

Pointers and Nodes

You might be wondering what an object actually is in a computer? In truth, there is no computer on Earth that knows what an object is, but they do know how to section off parts of memory (like with arrays). This is where objects live in computers, large chunks of memory. When we create an object like Lion *simba* = new Lion() what we are really doing is telling Java to make a chunk of memory big enough to hold our *Lion* class and store the location of that memory in our variable *simba*.

In Java, we call these variables references†. A reference is any variable that points to an object in memory. By using this fact to our advantage we can create more complex objects. On the next page is an example code that uses this feature

---

†: *Note For C and C++ Programmers:*

> *A reference is not the same thing as a pointer in C or C++. You can't preform arithmetic or other such operations on Java references. There are also other more complex reasons for this distinction that are beyond the scope of this book.*

```
public class Node {

    Node nextNode;
    int value;

    public Node ( int v, Node next ) {
          value = v;
    }

    public int getValue ( ) {
          return value;
    }

    public Node getNextNode ( ) {
          return nextNode;
    }

}
```

The constructor for this class takes in an integer for a value for the Node class to hold, and another Node object to be used as a reference. We could use a series of these Node object to create structures like in the following code:

```
public class MainClass{

  public static void main ( String [ ] args ) {

    Node nodeTwo = new Node ( 101, null );
    Node nodeOne = new Node ( 2, nodeTwo );
    Node nodeZero = new Node ( 15, nodeOne );

}
```

For node two we set its value to 101 and its reference to null (no value). The second node holds the value of 2 with a reference to the last node, and the first node holds 15 with a reference to node one. We represent this graphically like this

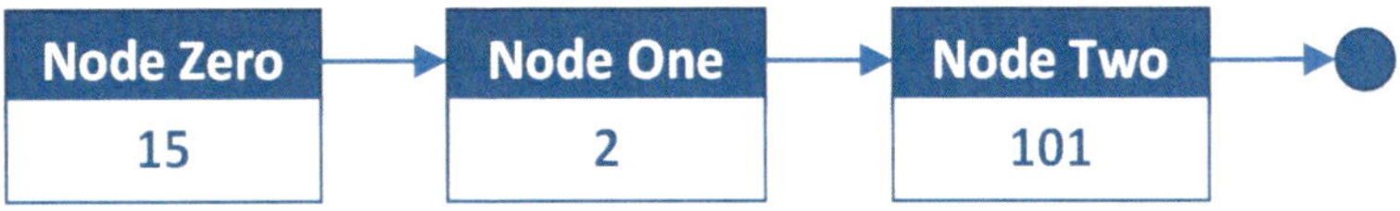

Where each box represents a node object and each arrow represents a reference. You will notice that node two points to a circle, this represents null. Although this might seem rather useless right now, by exploiting this concept we can obtain some very interesting behavior.

Stacks

A stack is a first-in-first-out data structure (abbreviated FIFO). This means that when an element is added to a stack it is also the first element out of the stack. You can think of a stack as a literal stack of objects. Each node in the stack references the object bellow it, and the only way to get to a lower object is to remove the ones on top of it. We represent a stack using the diagram to the right.

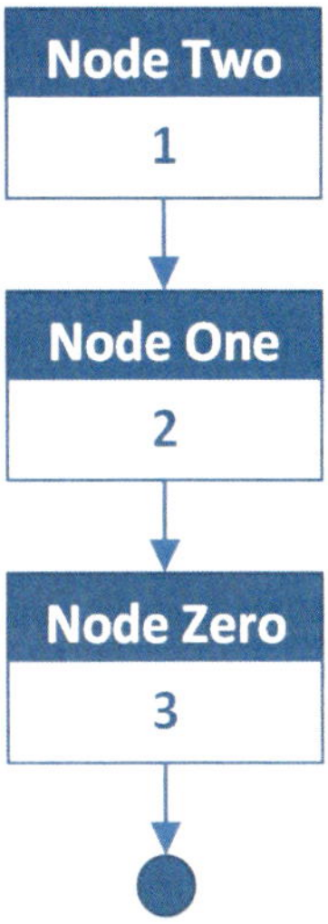

To access node two, you must first remove node one and follow its reference. This rule is what causes the FIFO behavior. You can think of stacks as storage devises that reverse the order you put things in. For example, if you put in 3, 2, 1 you will reverse the order when you take each of the number back out (1, 2, 3) because the stack is a FIFO structure.

Although you can make your own stack class, and all the methods required for it, Java already has one built. To use it just import it from java.util.Stack. Here is a sample code that reverses an array of characters.

```
Stack <Character> stack = new Stack <>( );
char [ ] a = { 'A', 'B', 'C', 'D', 'E', 'F' );

for ( int i = 0; i < a.length; i++ ) {
    stack.push( array [ i ] );
}

while ( !stack.isEmpty( ) ) {
    char temp = stack.pop ( );
    System.out.println( temp );
}
```

There are a few methods in the stack class that might have you a bit confused.

- push(element) - adds the given element to the top of the stack.

- pop( ) - returns the value of the top element and removes it from the stack.

- peek( ) - returns the value of the top node, but doesn't remove it (not used in this example).

- isEmpty( ) - returns true if the stack has no more nodes.

In addition, we had to use something that we have never used before when we created our stack, generics. Designated by the angled brackets (< >), generics are a very advanced object oriented programing tool that makes our code even more modular. They are too advanced to discuss in depth in this book. Just know that when we write: Stack<Character> stack = new Stack< >( ) we are telling Java that this stack stores characters. See the back of the "Useful Tables and References" for a list of commonly used generic types.

Array Lists

A second useful structure is the array list. In Java (and most programing languages) arrays have a fixed length. This makes them hard to use when you don't know how much data you have to store. Generally, programmers solve this problem by either making their arrays huge, or constantly making new arrays to fit their data. By using references and nodes, however, we can create a structure that can be used like an array and grows like a stack.

The following code stores the numbers one to ninety-nine in an array list.

```
ArrayList <Integer> list = new ArrayList <>( );

for ( int i = 0; i < 100; i++ ) {
    list.add( i );
}

for ( int i = 0; i < list.size( ); i++ ) {
    System.out.print( list.get( i ) + " " );
}
```

Just like with the stack, you will have to import the array list from java.util.ArrayList. Here are the basic methods in the array list class.

- add(element) - Adds the given element to the end of the array list.

- add(element, index) - Adds the given element to the array list, inserting it at the given index.

- get(index) - returns the element stored at the given index.

- size ( ) - returns the number of elements stored in the array list.

Object Structures - Exercises

1. How are objects stored in a computer's memory?

2. What is a pointer and how are they related to objects?

3. How do we represent a pointer graphically?

4. Draw a diagram that represents the following:

    - Node one points to Node two
    - Node two points to Node one
    - Node three points to Node one

5. What does FIFO stand for?

6. What is a stack?

7. If we put in "Alpha", "Beta", "Delta", "Gamma" into a stack what order would they come out in?

8. What does the following code print?

```
Stack <Double> stack = new Stack <>( );

stack.push( 10.00 );
stack.push( 21.34 );
stack.push( 39.12 );
stack.peek( );
stack.pop( );

System.out.println( stack.peek( ) );
```

9. What is a generic?

10. What is an array list?

11. What does the get( ) method do in an array list?

12. Array lists and stacks are not the only types of structures that can be created in Java. A queue is another type of structure that is first-in-first-out (FIFO). Describe how you think a queue works.

Chapter Ten:
User Input

Doing simple calculations and using pre-determined data can be useful, however the majority of your programs will run based off of some sort of user input. User input can be anything, from a key press, to a mouse movement, to entering data, answering prompts, and allowing what you type in to be manipulated by your code. In this chapter, we will be looking into using a scanner in order to read in inputs such as strings, integers, and doubles, and how to store them in your code and manipulate them.

When setting up user input, you have to use a scanner. A scanner is an object from the utilities library, that is imported from java.util.Scanner. To begin, we have to declare our import, directly above where you create your class.

```
import java.util.Scanner;

public class UserInput {

}
```

Now that we have our import, we are free to create the scanner. To create the scanner, we must first create a public method like what is shown below.

```
import java.util.Scanner;

public class UserInput {

  public static void main( String [ ] args ) {

  }
}
```

Inside the main method, we create our scanner using the line:

```
Scanner name = new Scanner( System.in );
```

In this line, Scanner is the type of the object, name is the name of the scanner which follows the rules of variable names, new is the keyword that says that this object has never been created before with this name, so it is brand new, we declare the type again, saying that it is a new object of type scanner, and then System.in means that we are taking in inputs from the console. Later in this chapter, we will be looking at what it means when reading an input from a file, and what the differences are.

Now that we have created a scanner object, we have to give it an action so that it will actually perform the tasks that it needs to. The object class Scanner has many different methods that we can call upon, however the ones that we will be looking at are what follows:

- next( ) - reads in the next input that is a string, stops at all spaces and line breaks.

- nextInt( ) - reads in the next input that is an integer, stops at all spaces and line breaks.

- nextDouble( ) - reads in the next input that is a double, stops at all spaces and line breaks.

- nextLine( ) - reads in the next input that is a string, stops at all line breaks but not spaces.

- hasNext( ) - normally used in a while loop or an if statement. It will return true if there is more text to read, and false otherwise.

In order to call upon these methods, if you remember back to the objects and inheritance chapter, in order to call upon a method from another class, we use: *objectName.method( );*

Something to remember is that each object will store its own data in the different methods, so if you had two different objects, and stored your data in them, the data can only be called from the same object. This means that *object1.getData( )* gets the data for *object1* and only *object1*, and *object2.getData( )* gets the data for *object2* and only *object2*.

Say you wanted to read in an integer of your choosing and then manipulate it. What method would we use? We would use nextInt( ) to get the integer that we are putting in and store it into the type integer, so that the types match as so:

```
import java.util.Scanner;

public class UserInput {

   public static void main( String [ ] args ) {

      Scanner name = new Scanner ( System.in );
      System.out.println( "Enter an integer: " );
      int x = name.nextInt( );
      name.close( );

   }

}
```

This code creates a new scanner, and then says that the integer x is equal to whatever integer you put into the console. For example, if you put in 9, x would be set equal to 9.

An important thing to remember is to always close the scanner. This is important, because if you are trying to do other things in the code, it uses a ton of memory, which can slow down the computer, and it is also extremely unsafe. It leaves open a part of your code that hackers and other people can get into and manipulate your code, making it so that the data that is stored is unsafe, exposed, and can be easily compromised.

Now say that you wanted to manipulate the data. To manipulate it, you would just take whatever variable you stored your input in, and manipulate that as you would a normal variable.

For example, say *x* was still 9, and you ran the code below, the console would then print out 27.

```
import java.util.Scanner;

public class UserInput {

  public static void main( String [ ] args ) {

    Scanner name = new Scanner ( System.in );
    System.out.println( "Enter an integer: " );
    int x = name.nextInt( );
    System.out.println( 3 * x );
    name.close( );

  }

}
```

While this is all good for taking in one input, say we wanted the program to repeat indefinitely, so it would restart the scanner every time until either a command was typed in that broke the loop, or just run infinitely. We would use an infinite *for* loop for this. One of these loops looks like:

```
for ( ; ; ) {
    .
    .     //Code for the scanner and print lines
    .
}
```

This *for* loop, as it is now, would run forever, until you physically stopped the program.

The infinite *for* loop works for simple operations such as wanting to take a sum of all of the inputs until -1 is entered, and then the code prints out the sum and the average?

```
import java.util.Scanner;

public class UserInput {

   public static void main( String [ ] args ) {

      Scanner name = new Scanner ( System.in );
      int n = 0;
      int x = 0;
      int sum = 0;

      for ( ; ; ) {
         System.out.print( "Enter a number: " );

         x = scan.nextInt( );
         if ( x == -1 ) {
            break;
         } else {
            sum += x;
            n++;
         }
      }
      double avg = ( double ) sum / n;
      System.out.println( "Sum " + sum );
      System.out.print( "Average " + avg + "\n");
      scan.close( );
   }

}
```

In the code on the left, the *for* loop will run until -1 is typed in, causing the code to break out of the loop. An important thing to note, is we created all of our variables outside the loop. This way we were able to continuously add to them, instead of them turning back to 0 every time the loop restarted.

There is another way to provide data and other information to the program that you are working on. This way of providing information is through having your code scan through a file, and then performing the same tasks of manipulation that you can use when you do user inputs through the console.

It is also important to point out that *for (; ;)* is equivalent to *while (true)*. Either one of these will create an infinte loop.

Using Files as Input:

To do this, first we need to make an empty text file within the project. To do this, right click on the project folder, select new, and then file. Then name your file test.txt. Make sure that the file you created is inside the project folder and not in the source folder. Inside the file write the numbers 5 and 6 with a space between them.

Now you are ready to start coding!

Remember how when we made a scanner we used the System.in command? To use a file as the input, all we have to do is replace that with a file object so it looks like:

```
File file = new File( "test.txt" );
Scanner scan = new Scanner( file );
```

Keep in mind that we may have to import the file object and the file not found exception from java.io

For our first example, let's create:

- A static method called scanInput that returns an int.
- Then, use the 2 lines of code above and create a new file and a scanner.
- Use a while loop to make the scanner read in more data while scanner still has something left to read.
- Add each integer read from the file to your total.
- Then close the scanner and return the total.

```
public static int scanInput( ) {
    int total = 0;

    try {

          File file = new File( "test.txt" );
          Scanner scan = new Scanner( file );

          while ( scan.hasNext( ) ) {
                total += scan.nextInt( );
          }
          scan.close( );

    } catch ( FileNotFoundException e ) {
          e.printStackTrace( );
    }

    return total;

}
```

What this method does when called upon is create a new file, a new scanner, and a new variable called total which adds up every int that is read in by the scanner and stores it. Once the scanner runs out of input, it closes the scanner for safety reasons, and returns the total.

You will notice that all of this is surrounded in a try-catch block. A try-catch block is a special section of code that surrounds sections of code that might throw errors. In this example Java could try to load the file and find that it is not there. This would cause a FileNotFoundException to be thrown. If the try-catch block was not present to "catch" the exception then our code would crash.

In general a try-catch block looks like this:

```
try {
    //Section of code that might throw an error
} catch ( ExeptionThatWilBeThrown e ) {
    // What we want to do is the error occurs
}
```

In our example we put all our scanner and file IO in the try section, because it could throw errors. In the catch section we wrote:

```
e.printStackTrace();
```

This will print the error to the console without crashing the program. We often include this line in try-catch blocks to make debugging easier.

Try making a main method that calls upon this method with your text file, and see what you get!

User Input- Exercises

1. What is user input and why is it useful?

2. What is a scanner?

3. List the five primary methods used in a scanner and what they do.

4. Why is it important to close the scanner after we are done using it?

5. What is the new line character?

6. In previous chapters, it was stated that infinite loops should always be avoided. How and why are they used in user input, and how do we make them safe to use?

7. Describe what the following code does.

```
public static void main( String [ ] args ) {
    Scanner scan = new Scananer( System.in );
    int num = 0;
    for ( ; ; ) {
          num = scan.nextInt( );
          if ( num == -1 ) {
                break;
          } else if ( num % 2 == 0 ) {
                System.out.println( num + " E");
          } else {
                System.out.println( num + " O");
          }
    }
    System.out.println( "END" );
    scan.close( );
}
```

8. Modify the code in number seven to find the largest number of the entered values and print it at the end.

9. How do you create a text file (.txt) in Java?

10. What is a try/catch block, and what is it used for?

11. What is the FileNotFoundException?

Chapter Ten:
Java FX

So far in your programing experience you have used the console to interact with your programs, taking in user input and printing our various things. However, this is not how most programs interact with people. The vast majority of programs (internet browsers, text editors, operating systems, etc.) have windows, buttons, sliders, and other graphics that make it easy to interact with the program. In this chapter, you will learn the basics of how to do just that by using JavaFX.

Before we get started here is some terminology that will be used:

- User - A person who will use our program.

- Graphical User Interface (GUI) - Often just called a GUI (pronounced Gooey), the GUI is the collection of windows, buttons, etc. that allow users to interact with our program without using the console.

So, what is JavaFX exactly? JavaFX is a collection of objects that allow us to easily create GUIs using the concepts of inheritance and object oriented design.

Eclipse and JavaFX

If you are using Eclipse to program then you will have to preform one extra step before you can use JavaFX. You will have to install e(fx)clipse before you can continue with this chapter.

1.) In Eclipse go to Help → Install New Software
2.) In the drop down select the version of Eclipse you are using.
3.) In filter type "e(fx)clipse".
4.) Once it loads, select e(fx)clipse.
5.) Click next and follow the rest of the installation instructions

Create Your First GUI

1. Make a new Java project.

3. Create a new Class and name it "FXExample".

4. Make your class inherits from Application:

```
public class FXExample extends Application {
```

5. There will be an error in your program because Java doesn't know what an application is. To fix this hover your mouse over the word "Application" and select: Import 'Application' (Javafx. application). In this chapter it is important that you only import objects from Javafx, not form sun or swing. Importing the wrong one will cause major bugs in your program

6. Once Application is imported you will get another error, this time because your class doesn't have a required method. So, we will have to add it. Change your code to look like this:

```
public class FXExample extends Application {

    public static void main( String [ ] args ){

    }

    @Override
    public void start ( Stage arg0 ) {

    }
}
```

Notice that in addition to overriding the start method (the method that needed to be included) we have also added the main method to our program.

7. Under our main method write:

```
public static void main( String [ ] args ) {
    launch( args );
}
```

This line of code is what tells JavaFX to start running. Without it, our program won't work.

8. Under the start method, write the following:

```
@Override
public void start( Stage arg ) {
    Pane root = new Pane( );
    Button btn = new Button( );
    btn.setText( "Say 'Hello World'" );
    root.getChildren( ).add( btn );

    arg.setScene( new Scene(root, 300, 250) );
    arg.setTitle( "Hello World!" );
    arg.show( );
}
```

NOTE: Depending on what version of Eclipse you are using the variable arg might be named something different.

So, what does this all mean? The first line creates something called the pane. The next three lines in the main method create a button and set the text on the button to be "Say 'Hello World!' " and add the button to the pane. The final three lines create the actual window by making a new scene, setting the title of the window, and finally the showing the window. If you run the code a new window like the one on the next page will pop-up.

Now, let's talk about the different parts of a window. There are three main parts of a window in JavaFX: the stage, scene, and pane. The stage is the actual window. Its job is to create a place that we can display things on (just like a theatre stage in real life). The scene is responsible for keeping track of what is currently being displayed. The pane (often called the root) is where all the action happens. This is where you put all the buttons, textfields, and animations. Together these three parts create the backbone of a functioning GUI.

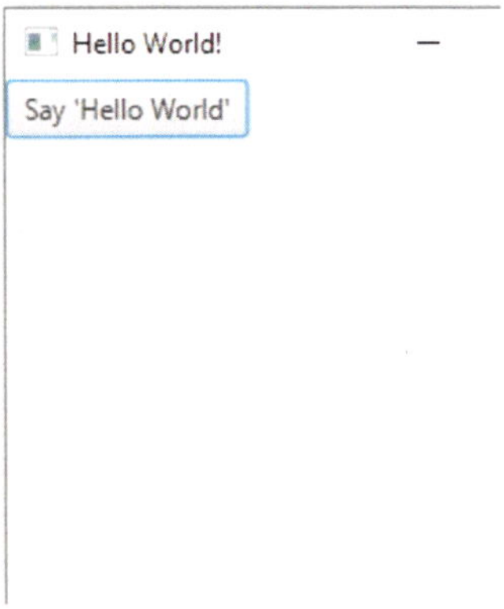

However, to make the GUI do anything you need to add nodes to the pane. Nodes are specialized objects like buttons, shapes, or text that can be added to the pane to change how the window looks or interacts.

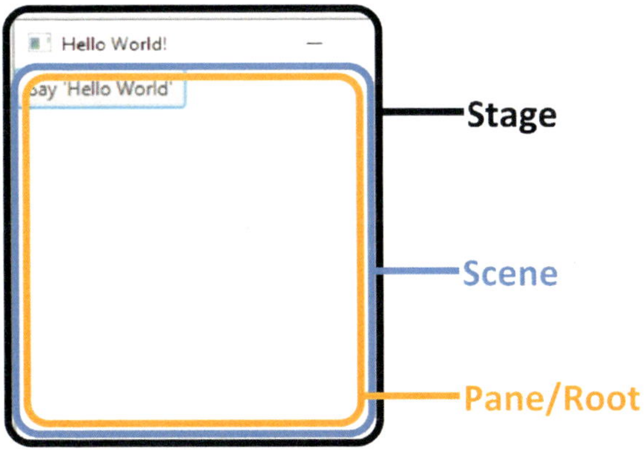

However, to make the GUI do anything you need to add nodes to the pane. Nodes are specialized objects like buttons, shapes, or text that can be added to the pane to change how the window looks or interacts.

User Interactivity and Event Handlers

Looking back at our example, the GUI we created doesn't do much at all. It just creates a window with a single button that doesn't do anything when it's clicked. To make our GUI interactive with the user (make it do something based on input), we must learn about a new type of method called event handlers.

Event handlers are methods that run only when a certain thing happens (someone clicks a shape, enters text, or press a button for example). Unlike the basic methods that we have used before these ones aren't called directly. For example, let's say we want the text "Hello World!" to appear on the screen when we click our button. To do this we would write the following code. Remember to always import from JavaFX. Compare your code to the new version below

```
public class FXExample extends Application {
  boolean btnPushed = false;

  public static void main( String [ ] args ){
    launch( args );
  }

  @Override
  public void start( Stage arg ) {
    Pane root = new Pane( );
    Label text = new Label( "Hello World!" );
    text.setTextFill( Color.BLUE );
    text.setLayoutX( 100 );
    text.setLayoutY( 100 );
    Button btn = new Button( );
    btn.setText( "Say 'Hello World'" );
    btn.setOnAction( new
      EventHandler<ActionEvent>( ) {
```

```
        @Override
        public void handle( ActionEvene event ) {
            if ( btnPushed == false ) {
              root.getChildren( ).add( text );
              btnPuched = true;
            }
        }
    });

    root.getChildren( ).add( btn );

    arg.setScene( new Scene(root, 300, 250) );
    arg.setTitle( "Hello World!" );
    arg.show( );
}
```

Let's walk through these new objects and methods one at a time. A label is a simple object that that can store a string which is displayed using whatever font, font size, and color you tell it to use. In this example, we set the label's x and y position in the window. Remember that in computer graphics the x and y axis are different from in a math class, meaning that the top left corner of the grid is (0, 0). As you move down your y value increases, moving left increases you x value.

The next part of the added code is the event handler. The first line tells the button to call the handle method whenever the button is pressed. The handle is just a simple if statement that adds the text label to the root pane. We need an if statement so we don't accidently add the same node twice to the pane.

Now that we have added functionality to our button, let's add a text field to our window. A text field is a simple element where a user can input a string which our program can treat like a variable. In this example, we will just display an input string as a label on our window by adding the following lines of code to our start method.

Add this code to the run method.

```
Label message = new Label ( "" );
message.setTextFill( Color.GREEN );
message.setLayoutX( 0 );
message.setLayoutY( 200 );
root.getChildren( ).add( message );

TextField txtField = new TextField( );
txtField.setLayoutX( 0 );
txtField.setLayoutY( 150 );
root.getChildren( ).add( txtField );

Button getText = new Button( );
getText.setText( "Get Text" );
getText.setLayoutX( 0 );
getText.setLayoutY( 175 );
getText.setOnAction( new
        EventHandler<ActionEvent>( ) {
    @Override
    public void handle( ActionEvent event ) {
        message.setText( txtField.getText( ));
    }
});
root.getChildren( ).add( getText );
```

Whenever the "Get Text" button is pressed the label will be changed to be whatever text the user entered. Try changing some of the code and customize the GUI. Can you change the text color? Font? Try changing what the buttons do.

Adding Shapes

Besides text fields, buttons, and labels you can also add shapes to windows. To begin, we will create a new project just like we did earlier in the chapter. We will also add the three basic components of a window (the pane, scene, and stage) at the beginning so we get a program that looks like this:

```
public class Shapes extends Application {
  public static void main( String [ ] args ) {
    launch( args );
  }

  @Override
  public void start( Stage arg ) {
    Pane root = new Pane( );
    arg.setTitle( "Shapes" );
    arg.setScene( new Scene( root, 300, 250 ));
    arg.show( );
  }
}
```

JavaFX's libraries include three basic shapes that will be discussed in this book: lines, circles, and rectangles. Adding a line is as easy as picking two points in the window. The line object will tell JavaFX to draw a line connecting those two points. Circles are defined by their center point and a radius. While rectangles are defined by their top left point, a width, and a height. Here is an example that does the following:

- Create a new line connecting points (20, 20) and (100, 100). Set its color to red.
- Create a new circle at point (200, 200) with a radius of 30, and set its color to be lime green.
- Create a new Rectangle with an upper left corner at (150, 100) with a width of 100 and height of 50. Set its color to be magenta.

```
@Override
public void start( Stage arg ) {
    pane root = new Pane( );

    Line line = new Line( 20, 20, 100, 100 );
    line.setStroke( Color.RED );
    root.getChildren( ).add( line );

    Circle c = new Circle( 200, 200, 30 );
    c.setFill( Color.LIMEGREEN );
    root.getChildren( ).add( c );

    Rectangle r = new Rectangle( 150, 100, 100,
          50);
    r.setFill( Color.MAGENTA );
    root.getChildren( ).add( r );

    arg.setTitle( "Shapes" );
    arg.setScene( new Scene( root, 300, 250 ));
    arg.show( );
}
```

Adding Animation

JavaFX also allows us to do simple animations. For this first example, we will make our circle from the previous example bounce back and forth on the screen. To do this, we will first have to change where define our circle. Any object you want to animate must be defined at as a class variable (i.e. they must be at the top of your class not in a method.

To animate in JavaFX, an animation timer must be used. This timer will perform some action on at a rate of about 60 times per second. Here is our code with the animation timer added.

The code on the next page shows this change. Notice that although the circle is defined at the top of the class, we still set its color and add it to the root using the start method.

```
public class Shapes extends Application {
  Circle c = new Circle( 200, 200, 30 );
  public void start( Stage arg ) {
    pane root = new Pane( );

    Line line = new Line( 20, 20, 100, 100 );
    line.setStroke( Color.RED );
    root.getChildren( ).add( line );

    c.setFill( Color.LIMEGREEN );
    root.getChildren( ).add( c );

    Rectangle r = new Rectangle( 150, 100, 100,
          50);
    r.setFill( Color.MAGENTA );
    root.getChildren( ).add( r );

     AnimationTimer t = new AnimationTimer( ) {
       @Override
       public void handle( long now ) {

       }
     };

    arg.setTitle( "Shapes" );
    arg.setScene( new Scene( root, 300, 250 );
    arg.show( );
    t.start( );
  }
}
```

The first few lines of new code create a new animation timer that handles animation events. The middle part of the handle method is where our animation code will go. The last part of the code (timer.start()) starts the animation. Now that we know what each part does let's add some animations by changing the handle method.

```
public class Shapes extends Application {
  Circle c = new Circle( 200, 200, 30 );
  double speed = 5;
  public void start( Stage arg ) {
    pane root = new Pane( );

    Line line = new Line( 20, 20, 100, 100 );
    line.setStroke( Color.RED );
    root.getChildren( ).add( line );

    c.setFill( Color.LIMEGREEN );
    root.getChildren( ).add( c );

    Rectangle r = new Rectangle( 150, 100, 100,
         50);
    r.setFill( Color.MAGENTA );
    root.getChildren( ).add( r );

    AnimationTimer t = new AnimationTimer( ) {
      @Override
      public void handle( long now ) {
        if (c.getCenterX( ) <= 30 ||
              c.getCenterX( ) >= 270 ) {
              speed *= -1;
        }
        c.setCenterX( x.getCenterX( ) + speed);
      }
    };

    arg.setTitle( "Shapes" );
    arg.setScene( new Scene( root, 300, 250 ));
    arg.show( );
    t.start( );
  }
}
```

The speed variable controls how fast the ball bounces on the screen, while the if statement controls which direction the ball moves. Whenever it gets close to the edge of the window it switches the direction of the balls movement by multiplying the speed by negative one. The last part, changes the current center of the circle to a new point.

JavaFX- Exercises

1. What does GUI stand for?

2. What is JavaFX?

3. What are the three parts of every JavaFX window, and what does each part do?

4. What is a node?

5. What is an event Handler?

6. Explain the coordinate system used in GUI design.

7. In the following code, what does the button do when it is pushed?

```
Button btn = new Button( );
    btn.setText( "ECHO" );
    btn.setOnAction( new
          EventHandler<ActionEvent>( ) {

          @Override
          public void handle( ActionEvent e ) {
                String echo = "Echo!";
                int i = 10;
                while ( i > 0 ) {
                      System.out.println( echo );
                      i -= 2;
                }
          });
}
```

8. What is the difference between a label and a text field? What does each one do?

9. What are the three basic shapes available in JavaFX? How are each of them defined?

10. Why do animated objects have to be defined as static?

11. What is the animation timer? How do you use it?

12. When we create our moving circle, why do we need to multiply the speed by negative one occasionally?

13. Write code to make the circle bounce diagonally. (Hint: does the circle's x-coordinate, y-coordinate, or both change over time?)

(Note: there is no answer in the back of the book for this question).

Style Guide

Naming Conventions:

Projects:

- Name should begin with an uppercase letter (ex. Game).
- The first letter of every word in the name should be uppercase (ex. MyFirstGame).
- No spaces or special characters (@, #, _, -, ...).
- Avoid using numbers (i.e. use "One" instead of "1").
- Try to keep it short and relative to what the project does.

Packages:

- Naming convention is similar to projects but should use lower case letters.

Classes:

- Naming Convention is similar to projects.

Methods:

- Name should begin with an lowercase letter (ex. run( )).
- The first letter of every word after in the name should be uppercase (ex. runGame( )).
- No spaces or special characters (@, #, _, -, ...).
- Avoid using numbers (i.e. use "One" instead of "1").
- Try to keep it short and relative to what the project does.

Variables:

- Naming convention is similar to methods

Comments:

- There should be a header in each class file listing the author(s), date the class was last modified, and a short description of what it does. Occasionally, the header will also include the programmer's contact information.

- Describe what each variable does when it is first used.
- Place a comment before each method to describe what it does.
- Additional comments can be used to explain more complex sections of code, but try to keep them short and to the point.
- Don't repeat comments.

Use of Spaces:

- There should always be a space after a opening parenthesis ("(") and a space before a closing parenthesis (")"). For example: int a = (4 + 5)
- The rule for parentheses applies to square brackets([ ]), but not to the angle brackets (< >) used for generics.
- There should be a space before and after every mathematical operator.
- A space should be placed after the words if, else , for, and while when creating if statements or loops.

Use of Mathematical Parentheses:

- Use parentheses whenever the order of operations matter. Do not rely on Java to use the correct order of operations.

Use of Braces:

- There are two main styles for bracing you can use whichever one you like, but you can't switch between the two styles in the same program.

K & R

```
if ( num <= 0 ) {
    num++;
}
```

Allman

```
if ( num <= 0 )
{
    num++;
}
```

Useful Tables and References

Table 1: Class Access Modifiers

Modifier	Description
default*	This class can only be accessed by classes within the same package
public	This class can be accessed by any other class

Table 2: Class Non-Access Modifiers

Modifier	Description
abstract	This class must be inherited. You can't use this class only its children.
final	This class can't be inherited

Table 3: Method Access Modifiers †

Modifier	Description
default*	This method can only be used (accessed) by classes in the same package
private	This method can only be used (accessed) by the class it is located in
protected	This method can only be used by classes in the same package or children of this class.
public	This method can be used (accessed) by any class

Table 4: Method Non-Access Modifiers †

Modifier	Description
abstract	You must override this method in a child class in order to use it.
final	This is the final version of the method and it can't be overwritten
static	For all practical purposes this makes it so that there can only be one method with this name in your class.

Table 5: Variable Access Modifiers †

Modifier	Description
default*	This variable can only be used (accessed) by classes in the same pacakge
private	This variable can only be used (accessed) by the class it is located in
protected	This method can only be used by classes in the same package or children of this class.
public	This variable can be used (accessed) by any class

Variable 6: Variable Non-Access Modifiers †

Modifier	Description
final	This is the final version this variable and it can't be changed
static	For all practical purposes this makes it so that there can only be one variable with this name in your class.

Table 7: Special Characters

Special Charcter	What is Printed
\"	Double Quotation Mark
\'	Single Quotation Mark
\\	Back Slash
\n	New Line
\t	Tab
\b	Backspace
\r	Carriage Return

---

* : *If no access modifier is defined for a class, method, or variable, then Java will automatically assign it the default modifier.*

† : *Not all modifiers have been included as some are too advanced to explain in this introductory book.*

Table 8: Variable Types

Name	What it Holds
byte	A single byte, a number between 127 to -128.
short	Whole numbers between 32,767 to -32,768.
int	Whole numbers between -2,147,483,648 and 2,147,483,647. You should always use this over byte, short, and long unless you either need a larger number or you need to be concerned about memory usage.
long	Whole numbers between -9,223,372,036,854,775,808 and 9,223,372,036,854,775,807. The long takes up more space than the int, only use it when necessary
float	A decimal number with about 6 significant digits.
double	A decimal number with about 15 significant digits. Although a double takes up more space than a float, you should always use a double unless you have a good reason not to.
boolean	True or False
char ‡	A single ASCII character
String	A series of char(s)

Table 9: Common Generic Types §

Generic Type	What it Holds
<Integer>	int
<Double>	double
<Boolean>	boolean
<Character>	char
<String>	String

---

‡ : *Remember that all ASCII values are stored as whole numbers. So adding one to the letter "a" will give you "b".*

```
char letter = 'a';
letter += 1;
System.out.println( letter );
```

Prints "b"

§ : *Any object can be used as a generic type. For example, ArrayList<Lion> would make an array list that holds our Lion class from chapter seven.*

How to Download Java

For Windows:

1. Go to the Java SE download site.
2. Find the latest version of Java SE and choose JDK.
3. Choose the correct download for your operating system:
    - "Windows x64" for 32 bit operating systems.
    - "Windows x86" for 64 bit operating systems.
4. Run the download installer, and accept all defaults.
5. Launch the: Control Panel → System → Advanced Settings
6. Under "System Variables", scroll down to "Path" and select "Edit"

For Windows 10:

I. You should see a table listing all path variables.
II. Click "New" and enter the path to the JDK's bin directory By default the will be something like: "c:\Program Files \Java\jdk1.#.#_##\bin" where # depends on the version.
III. Select "Move Up" to move the new path variable to the top.

For OS Prior to Windows 10:

I. READ ALL STEPS THIS CAN'T BE UNDONE.
II. Copy all text in "Variable Value" into a text file in case you mess up.
III. At the beginning of the text write the path to the JDK's bin directory. By default the will be something like: "c:\ Program Files\Java\jdk1.#.#_##\bin" where # depends on the version.
IV. Follow the path with a semicolon (;).
V. Do NOT delete any other entries. If you do copy the old text back in and start over.

8. Unzip the download files into the directory you want to store your program files in.

For Mac OS:

1. In some Mac systems the JDK is already installed. To check search for “Terminal” and run the terminal.

2. Run this command: `Javac -version`
   If a version number is returned then you already have the JDK installed. Otherwise continue to step three.

3. Go to the Java SE site and download the latest JDK for Mac OS.

4. Double click on the downloaded file and follow the instructions.

Answers

Chapter 1:

1. A computer is any device that can store and manipulate data.

3. Machine language uses only 1s and 0s and is very difficult for programers to understand.

5. Package Explorer, the Editor Window, and the Console

7. public - The method can be used by any class.
   private - The method can only be used by the class that created it.

9. Modifiers - Tell the compiler what the method can and can't do
   Return Type - The output of the method.
   Name - the name of the method.
   Arguments - The inputs to the method.

Chapter 2:

1. A variable is any type of data that can store a specific value.

3. A) Decimal Numbers
   B) Single Character
   C) True or False
   D) A Whole Number
   E) A Series of Characters

5. num++ increments the variable num by 1 (i.e. it adds 1 to num).

7. It prints: 9

9. A) 1 B) 2 C) 0 D) 0 E) undefined

Chapter 3:

1. A boolean expression is a set of variables and operators that evaluate to either true or false.

3. A) True B) True C) False D) True

5. (num % 17) == 0

7. It prints: Even

Chapter 4:

1. A loop is a section of code that is done repeatedly until a certain condition is met.

3. An infinite loop is any loop that will go on forever . They are dangerous because, by definition, they never end and can cause unpredictable behavior.

5. It prints the numbers 100, 80, 60, 40 and 20 on separate lines.

7. A *do while* loop has one boolean condition that is cheaked after the loop is executed. This means that a the loop will always execute at least once.

9. num++ increments after the loop executes. ++num increments before the loop executes.

Chapter 5:

1. An array is a chunk of computer memory that is reserved for a certain type of variable.

3. 0

5. It prints: { 100, 68, 120, 68, 1960, 522 }

Chapter 6:

1. An array of chars.

3. A) char{ 'H', 'i' }
   B) char{ 'a', 'b', 'c', 'd', 'e', 'f', 'g', 'h, 'i', 'j', 'k' }
   C) char{ 'T', 'o', ' ', 'b', 'e', ' ', 'o', 'r', ' ', 'n', 'o', 't', ' ', '2', ' ', 'b', 'e', '?' }

5. It prints: TODAY IS sunny

Chapter 7:

1. A method is a small section of code that can be called form a larger program.

3. A) String B) double[ ] C) nothing

5. Methods help to organize code into sections that accomplish one task.

7. It prints: 10

9. The getS method is supposed to return a String but actually returns an int.

11. Infinite recursion can cause unpredictable behavior in a code.

Chapter 8:

1. An object is a collection of methods and variables

3. Answers will vary.

5. An arrow with a solid line and a outlined head.

7. The extends keyword is what causes inheritance in Java.

9. The dot operator is used to access methods and variables in other objects.

11. A constructor is a type of method that helps with initializing objects.

Chapter 9:

1. Objects are stored as designated blocks of memory.

3. A pointer is represented by an arrow.

5. First In First Out

7. “Gamma”, “Delta”, “Beta”, “Alpha”

9. A generic is designated by angled brackets (< >) and tells more advanced objects what type of variable to use.

11. The get method returns the element at the specified index.

Chapter 10:

1. User input is any data that is externally given to a program. It is used to control the functionality of a program dynamically.

3. next( ) reads in the next input that is a string, stops at spaces and line breaks. nextInt( ) does the exact same thing but reads in integers. The same is true for nextDouble( ) but it returns doubles. nextLine( ) reads the next input as a string and only stops at new lines. Finally, hasNext() returns true if there is something to read in.

5. The new line character ('\n') is used to start a new line of text.

7. The program reads in numbers from the user (printing if they are odd or even) until a negative one is entered.

9. Select New→ file in the project and name it with .txt

11. The FileNotFoundException is thrown whenever the given file does not exist.

Chapter 11:

1. Graphical User Interface

3. The stage is the actual window, the scene keeps track of what is being displayed, and the pane is where all displayed objects are stored.

5. Event Handlers are methods that run only when a certain thing happens.

7. The button prints "Echo!" five times.

9. The basic shapes are the Line (defined by two points), the rectangle (defined by a point, a length, and a width), and the circle (defined by a point and a radius).

11. The animation timer runs whatever is in its event handler every frame.

87034693R00060

Made in the USA
San Bernardino, CA
31 August 2018